DEDICATED TO THE STUDENT
at Sheridan Elementary School
in Orangeburg, SC,
who wanted to know if there were any
black heroes of the Revolutionary War

The illustrations are in colored pencil and gouache
Printed in the USA by Electric City Printing in Anderson, South Carolina

ISBN 0966711467

Published by Warbranch Press, Inc.
329 Warbranch Rd.
Central, SC 29630

First Printing

ALMOST INVISIBLE:
Black Patriots
of the
American Revolution

by
Kate Salley Palmer

WASHINGTON'S MIXED MULTITUDE

At the time of the Revolution, there were about 3 million people living in the American colonies. Almost 500,000 of these people were black. Only a few black people were free. The rest were slaves, prisoners of owners who treated them as property. It was against the law for slaves to be educated.

Most African Americans did not know how to read or write, so most of the history of that time has been told by white people. We know about African American patriots of the Revolutionary War only from things white people wrote, or from a few black patriots who could read and write. African American patriots of the Revolution have been almost invisible for many years.

African Americans fought in almost every major battle of the war. About 5,000 black soldiers fought in George Washington's Continental Army. Washington called it a "mixed multitude." Black soldiers ate, slept, marched, and fought side by side with white soldiers.

CRISPUS ATTUCKS

The first American patriot to die in the very first deadly clash of the Revolutionary War was a black man. His name was CRISPUS ATTUCKS. He was a runaway slave who had escaped to the sea and then settled in Boston. CRISPUS ATTUCKS was a large man, the son of a black father and a Native American mother of the Natick tribe. In the Natick language, "attuck" means "deer."

American Colonists were angry because they had to obey laws made for them in England.

British soldiers were stationed in Boston. On the clear, cold night of March 5, 1770, hard feelings between Bostonians and British soldiers exploded. A crowd of men and boys had gathered, throwing snowballs, rocks, and ice at the soldiers.

Bells began to ring, calling other Bostonians out. CRISPUS ATTUCKS appeared, carrying a long, sturdy piece of wood. He led a crowd up to the soldiers and yelled at them. The soldiers pointed sharp bayonets at the crowd. ATTUCKS angrily pushed aside a bayonet and struck at a British soldier with the piece of wood. The soldiers fired their guns, killing ATTUCKS and four other men.

CRISPUS ATTUCKS died first, with 2 musket balls in his chest. Colonists said the men who died were martyrs to the cause of freedom, and buried them all together in Boston's Middle Burying Ground. Years later, a monument was erected over the place where they were buried.

LEMUEL HAYNES

On April 19, 1775 just after 2 am, 700 British soldiers began marching to the Massachusetts villages of Lexington and Concord. They wanted to destroy all military equipment and supplies they could find. Drummers in every town called Minutemen to action. Colonists awoke and headed to Lexington and Concord. African Americans stood ready to fight beside their white neighbors.

LEMUEL HAYNES was there. He was a free man who loved to read and write poetry. HAYNES survived the fighting that day, and later, on May 10, 1775, LEMUEL HAYNES helped Ethan Allen of Vermont lead a small force of farmers called the "Green Mountain Boys" to capture Fort Ticonderoga, a stone-walled British stronghold on a cliff overlooking the Hudson River. Allen and the Green Mountain boys, with help from Benedict Arnold and some militiamen, crept up to the walls and found an unlocked gate. They were able to charge into the fort and capture it. After the War, LEMUEL HAYNES became an ordained minister with churches in Vermont and New York. He became one of the most popular ministers of his time.

PETER SALEM

PETER SALEM was at Lexington and Concord. He was a slave whose owners had freed him to fight. He also fought at the battle of Bunker Hill. The Patriots wanted two hills— Bunker's and Breed's—across the harbor from the city of Boston. They started building a redoubt (small fort) on Breed's Hill after dark on July 16, 1775. All night they worked with pickaxes and shovels, building walls of dirt and stone. They were still working when dawn came. British warships began firing at them. Fifteen hundred British troops came ashore in boats, and marched in straight lines up the hill. The militia and Minutemen on the hill didn't have much ammunition, so their officers told them not to fire at the British until they saw "the whites of their eyes." As the British began to overrun the fortification, PETER SALEM shot and killed an important British officer, John Pitcairn. The "PETER SALEM gun" is on display at the Bunker Hill monument today. He kept fighting to the end that day, barely escaping. Later, on July 30, 1777, SALEM was at the battle of Saratoga, using the same gun he had used at Bunker Hill. After the war, PETER SALEM returned to Massachusetts, built a cabin there, and wove cane for a living. In 1816, he died in the poorhouse.

BARZILLAI LEW

BARZILLAI LEW was a large black man who played the fife and drums. He helped Ethan Allen and the Green Mountain Boys capture Fort Ticonderoga. BARZILLAI LEW also fought at Bunker Hill, keeping American spirits high by playing "Yankee Doodle Dandy" on his fife. He survived the September 11, 1777 Battle of Brandywine and, after that, the terrible winter encampment at Valley Forge. After the War, he married and fathered a large family. Many members of his family became musicians and soldiers. BARZILLAI LEW'S descendents believe that he traveled to New York City and played at George Washington's first inauguration. His Bunker Hill powder horn is displayed at an African American museum in Chicago.

SALEM POOR

SALEM POOR, a free man, kept fighting to the end at Bunker Hill, barely escaping. He is believed to have killed a British officer named James Abercrombie. SALEM POOR fought so bravely that a petition signed by 14 American officers reported that he had "behaved like an experienced officer as well as an excellent soldier." He also survived the winter camp at Valley Forge and fought at Monmouth Courthouse on June 28, 1778. Although he was praised for his actions at Bunker Hill, there is no record that SALEM POOR was ever given any reward after the War.

JUDE HALL

JUDE HALL fought so well at Bunker Hill that the other soldiers called him "OLD ROCK." HALL was with George Washington when he made headquarters at Brooklyn Heights, New York, in August of 1776. Washington hoped to protect Manhattan Island and its harbor from the British. Washington's army was badly defeated in the next several battles. The British had paid German soldiers to fight with them. The Americans called them "Hessians." The American army was in trouble. Several thousand were taken prisoner, hundreds were killed or wounded, and thousands more died of disease or ran away. JUDE "OLD ROCK" HALL came through the fighting unharmed. He stayed with the army and survived the Battle of Brandywine. He fought with the Continental army for eight long years, and after the War, he went back home to his family in New Hampshire.

WILLIAM FLORA

On December 9, 1776 the British tried to capture a bridge over the Elizabeth River below Norfolk, Virginia. The colonists held the bridge as long as they could before retreating to fortifications they had built. A free black man, WILLIAM FLORA, was the last man to reach safety. He didn't leave his post until he had fired at the British eight times. Then, crossing over a plank to the fortification, he turned and pulled the plank after him so the British couldn't cross it. FLORA went on to serve in the Continental Army throughout the war. He was with the American troops at Yorktown, the last battle of the Revolutionary War, using the same weapon he had used at The Battle of Great Bridge.

WILLIAM FLORA, who, years later would volunteer to fight the British again in the War of 1812, settled down in Portsmouth, Virginia. There he became a well-to-do businessman and property owner. He bought his wife and children out of slavery.

AFRICAN AMERICANS IN THE ARMY

In the summer of 1775, the Continental Congress formed the American Continental Army. Even though black soldiers had fought in earlier battles, military leaders like General Horatio Gates made a new rule preventing the use of African Americans as soldiers. One reason The Continental Congress wanted to exclude the African American soldier was that slave owners regarded slaves as their property and they didn't want to lose them. Slave owners in the South were afraid to put guns in the hands of slaves. They worried that the slaves would use the guns against their masters.

Individual state militia and regiments, even in New England, passed laws forbidding black, biracial, or native American men from serving in the military.

Free African Americans and those who had been serving all along protested the new policy. In December 1775, George Washington ordered officers to re-enlist free black men. The army needed good men. Some Northern states began to relax the rules. At that time, New Hampshire began to allow slaves and free blacks to serve.

African Americans continued to be accepted into the Continental Army, but South Carolina and Georgia, with the highest slave populations, never did allow slaves to fight as soldiers in the War.

When the Declaration of Independence was adopted on July 4, 1776, it seemed to many people that the words "all men are created equal," did not apply to African Americans.

PRINCE WHIPPLE

By December 18, 1776, Washington was camped near Trenton, New Jersey. Worried that that his army needed a victory, he decided to attack the Hessians at Trenton on the day after Christmas. Many soldiers began crossing the Delaware River by boat. Washington crossed about 8pm, in a scene made famous in the painting, "Washington Crossing the Delaware."

Pictured in the boat, pulling on one of the oars, is PRINCE WHIPPLE. He was a slave serving in the army for the promise of freedom. His real name is unknown, but he was from Africa—the son of wealthy parents who had sent him to America to be educated. Instead he was sold as a slave.

PRINCE WHIPPLE was freed from slavery during the war.
He settled in Portsmouth, Virginia, where he died at the
age of thirty-two, leaving a widow and children.

TOBIAS GILMORE

TOBIAS GILMORE was also from Africa. He was a prince called Shillbogee Turry-Werry. He was auctioned to a Captain Gilmore and enlisted in the army to regain his freedom.

TOBIAS GILMORE would later become one of Washington's bodyguards. He was also with Washington at Brooklyn Heights, but came through the bloody fighting unharmed. After the War, GILMORE went back to his home in Taunton, Massachusetts.

He received some land and a cannon for his military service.

Every 4th of July, he took the cannon to Taunton Green and fired 14 shots—one for each of the American colonies and one for George Washington.

PRIMUS HALL

PRIMUS HALL was also with Washington at Brooklyn Heights, but came through unharmed. He was with the Army at Princeton, New Jersey on January 3, 1777, where the Americans were able to take British soldiers by surprise. The two armies—British and American—stood 30 yards apart and fired guns at each other. Then the British ran. The Americans chased the Redcoats. PRIMUS HALL chased several British soldiers and captured them all by himself.

OLIVER CROMWELL

OLIVER CROMWELL was a free farmer from New Jersey who fought throughout the war. He was with Washington's army at Brooklyn Heights and survived the terrible fighting. He crossed the Delaware with Washington and fought at Trenton and Princeton. At Princeton, CROMWELL joined in the chase when the British ran away, later telling a newspaper that they had "knocked the British about lively." He survived Valley Forge and fought at Brandywine. He fought at Yorktown and to his dying day, he claimed to have seen the last man killed at Yorktown. OLIVER CROMWELL was very proud that his discharge from the army was in George Washington's own handwriting. He received a Badge of Merit for six years of faithful service, and was given a yearly pension. He lived to be 100 years old.

BENJAMIN BANNECKER

The American army's encampment at Valley Forge became famous for the shortages and hardship the Americans suffered that cold winter. More than 2,000 of the men had no shoes, and the trail leading to Valley Forge was tinged with the blood from their feet.

Three thousand soldiers ran away from the army in the first three months of 1778. Another 1,000 were so sick they could not leave their huts.

Farmers wouldn't sell them food and merchants wouldn't sell them clothes because their Continental money wasn't worth as much as the gold the British paid.

But one farmer, a brilliant free African American mathematician and astronomer named BENJAMIN BANNECKER, smuggled food to the soldiers through the British lines. BANNECKER would later go on to publish his own almanacs and help survey the land for the nation's capitol at the District of Columbia.

"TACK" or "JACK" SISSON

On July 9, 1777, "TACK" or "JACK" SISSON (people disagree on the pronunciation of his name), an African American, performed an unusual task for the Americans. He was part of a volunteer commando force sent to capture the British General Richard Prescott from British headquarters at Newport, Rhode Island. SISSON steered one of the five rowboats silently past huge British ships in the harbor.

They landed near the house where Prescott was staying and SISSON, with two other men, entered the house. They found the General's bedroom locked. SISSON broke the door down with his head! There they informed the general that he was a prisoner.

The story of "TACK" or "JACK" SISSON'S adventure caused quite a lot of entertainment and merriment among the Americans. They even wrote poems and songs about it. SISSON later enlisted as a private in Colonel Christopher Greene's FIRST RHODE ISLAND REGIMENT, and served for the rest of the War.

EDWARD HECTOR

EDWARD HECTOR was a 33-year-old African American private in the 3rd Pennsylvania Artillery. During the American retreat at Brandywine, he was ordered to abandon his ammunition wagon and join the retreat. "The enemy shall not have my team," he replied, "I will save my horses or perish myself!" Hector gathered up guns dropped by fleeing Americans as he calmly left the field with his ammunition wagon. He saved his team of horses and his wagon that day, and was ready to go the next morning.

Forty years later, the Pennsylvania legislature gave him a $40 donation. It was only enough to bury the brave soldier.

JOHN PETERSON

JOHN PETERSON, an African American, was at the Battle of Saratoga. Later, in September 1780, he and his friend, Moses Sherwood, prevented a British spy, Major Andre, from getting back to his ship. Andre had just met with the American General Benedict Arnold, who, now a traitor, offered to give the American fortress of West Point to the British. From the hill where they were making cider, PETERSON and Sherwood saw a boatload of men from the British ship. The men in the boat were trying to get to shore to pick up

Major Andre. PETERSON and Sherwood shot at the boat. The sailors had to return to the ship. Then, many armed townsmen began firing cannons and guns at the ship, damaging it. The ship had to sail away, leaving Andre stranded on shore. Andre was captured and hanged as a spy. The papers he had hidden in his boots were taken to Washington. That's when Washington realized that General Benedict Arnold had betrayed his country.

PETERSON was held prisoner once on a British prison ship, *The Jersey*. He escaped by climbing down the anchor chain.

JOHN PETERSON was awarded a pension and given a house for helping expose the traitor, Benedict Arnold.

After the War, PETERSON, returned to Cortland, New York and lived in the house he had been given. He lived to be 103 years old.

THE FIRST RHODE ISLAND REGIMENT

Some officers wanted to use the struggle for independence to help end slavery. One of these was Colonel Christopher Greene, the cousin of General Nathanael Greene. Colonel Greene helped create one of the most unusual units in the Revolutionary War— the BLACK REGIMENT OF RHODE ISLAND. The Rhode Island Legislature agreed that slaves who joined this force would be "absolutely free" the minute they joined up. They would be entitled to the same privileges as white soldiers. The state paid slave owners full value for any slave who joined the army.

The official name of this unit was the FIRST RHODE ISLAND REGIMENT. It served for five years. The FIRST RHODE ISLAND REGIMENT contained more than 200 African Americans. They were the heroes of a battle at Newport, Rhode Island, where they bravely held back several thousand British troops.

The FIRST RHODE ISLAND REGIMENT was a small part of a much larger force that day, but they played an important role. A unit of scary-looking Hessians attacked them fiercely for almost four hours. A white soldier who fought near them told what happened: "Three times … were they attacked with such desperate valor and fury by well-disciplined and veteran troops and three times did they successfully repel the assault, and thus preserve our army from capture. They were brave, hardy troops."

The French General, the Marquis de Lafayette, declared the battle to be "the best fought action of the war."

On May 13, 1781, a group of enemy soldiers attacked the REGIMENT's position several miles above New York City. They broke into the headquarters of Col. Christopher Greene of the FIRST RHODE ISLAND REGIMENT. One man wrote, "Colonel Greene was cut down and mortally wounded; but the sabers of the enemy only reached him through the bodies of his faithful guard of blacks who hovered over him to protect him, and every one of whom was killed."

Many other members of the regiment were wounded or taken prisoner that day. Most of the prisoners were sold into slavery in the British West Indies.

Later, at the Battle of Yorktown, the surviving members of the FIRST RHODE ISLAND REGIMENT stood ready to fight again.

After the British surrendered, the Continental Army marched in review. An officer with the French army wrote in his diary that the FIRST RHODE ISLAND REGIMENT "was the most neatly dressed, the best under arms, and the most precise in all their maneuvers."

After the War, they received no pay for their service, but they had earned their freedom.

ATTUCKS COMPANY

There were about 755 African Americans in fourteen Continental Army brigades, but there were many black soldiers in four other brigades. The 2nd Pennsylvania brigade had 148 African Americans. Two Virginia brigades followed with 96 in one and 89 in the other.

One Connecticut company was called the "ATTUCKS COMPANY" because all its members were black. By the third year of the war, 1778, at least one out of every twenty men in the army was African American.

THE BUCKS OF AMERICA

John Hancock, one of America's founding fathers, honored one African American Regiment with its own flag. Little is known of THE BUCKS OF AMERICA, but they may have been a group organized to protect the city of Boston during the War. They marched into town to receive the flag from Hancock. The flag was made of silk and pictured a pine tree and a deer, or buck. John Hancock's initials were on the flag as well. Maybe they called themselves "bucks" because of Crispus Attucks.

AUSTIN DABNEY

AUSTIN DABNEY was a teenage former slave serving in his master's place. He joined the militia led by Colonel Elijah Clarke. Clarke's forces fought in many battles in South Carolina and Georgia, including he battle of Cowpens. On February 14, 1779, DABNEY was the only African American at the Battle of Kettle Creek in the North Georgia woods. Clark's forces defeated a large group of Tories (British Loyalists) in what one man said was the hardest battle ever fought in Georgia.

AUSTIN DABNEY'S heroism that day earned him praise and rewards. More than 50 years later, a Georgia governor wrote of DABNEY, "No soldier under Clarke was braver, or did better service during the Revolutionary struggle." At Kettle Creek, AUSTIN DABNEY was shot in the thigh and crippled. A white soldier named Harris nursed him back to health. DABNEY worked for the Harris family after that, even sending the oldest Harris son through college. Several years after the battle, the Georgia Legislature awarded AUSTIN DABNEY 112 acres of land for his "bravery and fortitude…in several engagements and actions" against the enemy.

OSCAR MARION

Partisan leaders in South Carolina fought against the British. The finest of these was General Francis Marion, the "Swamp Fox." African American soldiers served in Marion's militia. We don't know exactly how many and we know only a few of their names. One was Marion's servant, OSCAR MARION, who accompanied him and fought with him everywhere he went. A famous painting hangs in the US Capitol building showing Marion inviting a Tory officer to supper, and OSCAR cooking sweet potatoes.

AGRIPPA HULL

AGRIPPA HULL, a free man, was at the Battle of Saratoga in New York. He was an orderly to the Polish volunteer, General Count Taddeusz Kosciuszko. In 1781, at the bloody Battle of Eutaw Springs in South Carolina, he helped the surgeons. Later in 1781 at Yorktown, he and Count Kosciuszko were still with George Washington. After the War, Count Koscuiszko wanted to take AGRIPPA HULL to Poland with him. But HULL returned to his home in Stockbridge, Massachusetts, and adopted the child of a runaway slave.

When Count Koscuiszko returned to the United States in 1797, AGRIPPA HULL traveled to New York City, where the two had a pleasant reunion. During his visit, Count Koscuiszko was given some land in Ohio. He ordered that the land be sold and the money used to start a school for black children.

ANTIQUA

ANTIQUA, a slave, served as a spy behind enemy lines. He was praised by the South Carolina General Assembly for "his skill in procuring information of the enemy's movements and designs…he always executed the commission with which he was entrusted with diligence and fidelity and obtained very considerable and important information from within the enemy's lines, frequently at the risk of his life."

To reward him, the assembly freed his "wife named Hagar and her child" from slavery. ANTIQUA may have remained a slave, but his wife and child could never be sold away from him.

YOUNG AFRICAN AMERICAN BUGLER

British General Cornwallis sent Col. Banastre Tarleton and his Green Dragoons after
American General Daniel Morgan in South Carolina. The brutal, arrogant Tarleton caught
up with Morgan on January 17, 1781 in a clearing where cattle wandered in open cowpens,
near present-day Spartanburg, SC. The area was called "The Cowpens."
Both sides had about 1,100 men.
One of the American heroes was a YOUNG AFRICAN AMERICAN BUGLER "too small

to [use] a sword." When Col. William Washington was about to be killed by a British officer, the bugler wounded the officer with a shot from a pistol.

The Battle of Cowpens lasted almost two hours, and when it was over, Tarleton's force was defeated. He and his men fled for twenty miles before escaping.

GEORGE LATCHOM

In 1981, a group of British soldiers landed at Henry's Point, Virginia. A militia group led by Colonel John Cropper met them there. With Colonel Cropper that day stood GEORGE LATCHOM, a slave belonging to one of Cropper's neighbors. There was a fight, and the Americans retreated through a swampy area, chased by the British. Colonel Cropper sank into the mud up to his waist, and was about to be killed by a British soldier. GEORGE LATCHOM shot the closest soldier, and when the others held back, he clasped Col. Cropper under the arms, and dragged him out of the mud. Then he lifted the colonel to his shoulders and carried him to safety. Everyone was amazed at LATCHOM'S strength, for Cropper was a large man who weighed about 200 pounds.

Colonel John Cropper was so grateful that he bought
LATCHOM from his owner, freed him, and "befriended
him in every way for the rest of his life."

JORDAN FREEMAN and LAMBERT LATHAM

One of the forts attacked by Benedict Arnold before the Battle of Yorktown was Fort Griswold. British Major William Montgomery was in charge of the forces taking this fort. He tried to climb the wall and was killed by spears held by a white officer and a black soldier, JORDAN FREEMAN, who died that day defending the fort. Another African American soldier, LAMBERT LATHAM, also behaved bravely at Fort Griswold, "Loading and discharging his musket with great rapidity even after he had been severely wounded in one of his hands."

When the British finally got into the fort, the American commanding officer, Lt. Col. William Ledyard, gave his sword to a British officer. This was the custom. But the British officer took Ledyard's sword and killed him with it. LAMBERT LATHAM immediately bayoneted the British officer to death, and soon lay dead himself from bayonet wounds—stabbed by furious British soldiers. Patriot captives were then killed as well.

Almost 50 years later, a monument was erected near the site "In memory of the brave patriots who fell in the massacre at Fort Griswold." The names of the two black patriots were placed at the bottom, separated from the names of their white companions by the label "Colored Men."

JAMES ARMISTEAD

George Washington sent the 23 year-old Marquis de Lafayette south to Virginia to try to keep Virginia out of the hands of Lord Cornwallis and Benedict Arnold, who was now a Brigadier General in the British Army.

JAMES ARMISTEAD was a 21 year-old slave. He offered to risk his life by spying for Lafayette even though he was promised nothing in return.

JAMES ARMISTEAD went to Benedict Arnold's camp and volunteered to work there. He listened to the officers talking among themselves. Whenever he had information for Lafayette, he enlisted others to carry messages. Sometimes he went to Lafayette's camp himself.

"Often at the peril of his life [he] … kept open a channel of the most useful information of the most secret and important kind," read a petition that was approved years later by the Virginia General Assembly.

When Benedict Arnold went to New York City, ARMISTEAD went to Lord Cornwallis's camp. Cornwallis was the commander of all the British forces in America. ARMISTEAD even worked in Cornwallis's own tent. Cornwallis trusted JAMES ARMISTEAD so much that he asked him to spy on Lafayette! ARMISTEAD immediately reported this to Lafayette.

After the surrender of the British at Yorktown, Cornwallis visited Lafayette's headquarters and was amazed to see JAMES ARMISTEAD there, talking with Lafayette. He shook his head. He had thought ARMISTEAD was his spy.

After the War, JAMES ARMISTEAD took the name JAMES ARMISTEAD LAFAYETTE in honor of the man he so admired. He was held in slavery for several years even though Lafayette tried to get him freed.

The Virginia Legislature finally freed JAMES ARMISTEAD LAFAYETTE, and when the Marquis de Lafayette returned to the United States in 1824, the two old soldiers held a joyful reunion.

SAUL MATTHEWS

Another African American spy at this time was SAUL MATTHEWS, a slave and a private in the army. He risked his life to go into British forts and get information. MATTHEWS' work was so important to the Americans that Col. Josiah Parker of the Virginia militia said he deserved the applause of his country. More praise came from Lafayette, General Nathanael Greene, and Col. Peter Muhlenburg.

SAUL MATTHEWS remained a slave after the war. In 1792, he asked the Virginia Legislature for his freedom. In November of that year, "in consideration of the many essential services rendered to this Commonwealth during the late war," he was granted his "full liberty and freedom…as if he had been born free."

JAMES FORTEN

Prisoners were held on British ships in dark, diseased and overcrowded holds below the decks where the men froze in winter and suffered from the heat in summer. About 11,500 men died aboard prison ships during the War.

One of the prisoners aboard the ship *The Jersey* was a 15-year-old free African American named JAMES FORTEN. He had been a sailor on a ship that was captured by a British warship. Most black members of that ship's crew were sold into slavery in the West Indies. But FORTEN had become such good friends with the British captain's young son that the captain offered JAMES FORTEN a life of opportunity in England if he would reject the United States. "I am here a prisoner for the liberties of my country," FORTEN replied, "I never, never shall prove a traitor to her interests!" The captain transferred JAMES FORTEN to *The Jersey*. There FORTEN devised a plan to escape in a chest of old clothes that was going ashore. At the last minute, however, JAMES FORTEN gave up his place to a younger prisoner. He even helped carry the chest containing the other boy down the gangplank.

When JAMES FORTEN was finally released from the prison ship where he had been held, he walked home to Philadelphia. He went on to a long and celebrated career. He would become, among other things, an inventor and manufacturer. He donated money to charity as well.

PHILLIS WHEATLEY

PHILLIS WHEATLEY was the first African American and the first slave ever to publish a book of poetry in the United States. She was born in Africa and sold at a Boston slave market in 1761 when she was about seven years old. Mrs. Susannah Wheatley bought her. PHILLIS did not work with other slaves in the Wheatley household. She had asthma, and Mrs. Wheatley was afraid she would get sick if she got too cold or damp.

PHILLIS was educated in the Wheatley home, studying the classics and the Bible at an early age. She began to write poetry while still in her teens, and became well known for her writing. Respected townspeople in Boston visited with her, lent her books, and read her poetry.

In 1773, a London publisher produced a book of PHILLIS WHEATLEY's poems entitled ***Poems on Various Subjects, Religious and Moral***. She traveled to London that year and was there while her book was being sold. The book was very popular, and it made her famous. In the front of the book, there was a drawing of PHILLIS WHEATLEY. When PHILLIS was twenty-one, Mrs. Susannah Wheatley died. PHILLIS wrote that Mrs. Wheatley had been more a mother and a friend than a mistress. PHILLIS WHEATLEY continued to write poems and letters.

In 1776 PHILLIS WHEATLEY wrote a poem about George Washington. He liked it so much he invited her to meet with him. She later visited him at his headquarters and was courteously received.

In April 1778, she married John Peters, a respected man of color who studied law. But things did not go well for the Peters family. Three children were born, and two of them died. At one time, John Peters went to jail for debt while PHILLIS scrubbed and cleaned in a lodging house. But her writing never stopped. She continued to publish letters, eulogies and poems. She died in December 1784 at the age of thirty-one.

AFTER THE WAR

These are only a few of the brave African American patriots of the Revolutionary War. There are others of whom we know little, or know nothing. But they fought for the same ideals of freedom and liberty for which all patriots fought.

Although slavery was not ended until many years after the Revolutionary War, the seeds of freedom did begin to take root. Some things began to change in the North. African Americans called for their freedom—and many of them won it because of their service in the War. Churches and schools rose up for the African American population. Slavery in the North began to disappear. By 1800, the number of free blacks in the North had risen

from 14,000 to 100,000. In 1855 Harriet Beecher Stowe, a famous abolitionist, wrote that the African American patriots of the Revolution were unusually generous, because they fought for "a nation which did not acknowledge them as citizens and equals…"

"It was not for their own land that they fought," she said, "nor even for a land which had adopted them, but for a land which had enslaved them, and whose laws, even in freedom, … oppressed rather than protected. Bravery, under such circumstances," she wrote, "has a peculiar beauty and merit."

GLOSSARY

Abolitionist – someone who wanted to end the practice of slavery.

American Revolution – the name for the events, mostly military, of 1775-1783 in the American colonies that allowed American patriots to cast off British rule and establish the United States of America.

Ammunition – objects, usually containing lead, fired from weapons such as muskets, rifles or pistols.

Artillery – cannons or other large guns used in war.

Asthma – a health condition or sickness causing difficulty in breathing.

Bayonet – a sharp blade attached to the end of a musket and used for stabbing.

Biracial – describes a person whose parents are of different races.

Bugler - a person who plays a brass wind instrument that's used for military calls or signals in actual battle or in ceremonies.

Colonist – someone who lives in a newly settled area – early people in the South Carolina colony were called colonists.

Colony – a community of people in a land ruled by another country - before the Revolution, there were 13 colonies in America ruled by Britain's King George III.

Constitution – a set of governing values for a state or country accepted by a group, such as the Continental Congress.

Continental Army – the army of professional American soldiers created by the Continental Congress and commanded by General George Washington.

Continental Congress –government that led the American Revolutionary cause - the First Continental Congress consisted of representatives of all the 13 colonies, and met in Philadelphia in 1774 - the Second Continental Congress declared independence in 1776 and served the American cause until the end of the war.

Eulogy – something spoken or written in praise of a particular person after his/her death.

Fife – a small wind instrument, similar to a flute, that makes a shrill sound – usually played along with drums in military marches.

Fortification – a defensive structure, like a fort, used in war.

Free men or free blacks – African Americans who were not slaves, but still had few rights.

Hessians – soldiers from Germany hired by the British to fight against the American patriots.

Invisible – unseen.

Loyalists – citizens of the colonies who were loyal to the British government and opposed the Revolution – most were called Tories.

Militia – unpaid civilian soldiers, such as farmers, who volunteered to fight and defend their communities against British and/or Tory forces - usually served for short terms of duty.

Minutemen – militia groups, mostly in the northern colonies, organized to respond to military emergencies "at a minute's notice."

Musket – a front-loaded firearm with a smooth barrel – capable of rapid reloading and firing – fairly accurate to 100 yards.

Native Americans – refers to the people who lived in America before the colonists came - these people were sometimes called Indians - they lived in tribes or nations, such as the Cherokee and the Catawba in South Carolina.

Oppress –to use unjust or cruel treatment to keep human beings down.

Parliament – the government of Great Britain consisting of two houses – the House of Commons, who were elected, and the House of Lords, whose seats were inherited.

Partisan – an unusual American patriot fighter – using ambush and surprise against their enemies at night or before dawn.

Patriot –American who wanted independence from Great Britain.

Pension – a payment given to someone who has performed a service – such as paid to a retired soldier.

Provincial – refers to a group of soldiers from a particular region or colony.

Provisions – food, water, weapons and ammunition for the soldiers.

Redcoats – soldiers who fought for the British in the Revolutionary War - their uniform coats were red.

Redoubt – a temporary defensive structure, such as a dirt wall or ditch, serving as a fort.

Regiment – large group of soldiers fighting together.

Reinforcements – additional troops rushed to provide help in battle.

Rifle – a Revolutionary War weapon with a long barrel containing grooves that caused the ammunition to spin and fly accurately for up to 300 yards.

Siege – the surrounding of a fort or a city to prevent any movement of people in or out.

Traitor – someone who turns against or betrays his country.

BIBLIOGRAPHY

Bodie, Idella. *Brave Black Patriots*. Orangeburg, SC: Sandlapper Publishing Co. 2002.

Buckley, Gail. *American Patriots – The Story of Blacks in the Military from the Revolution to Desert Storm.* New York, NY: Random House Trade Paperbacks. 2001.

Cooper, William J., Jr. *Liberty and Slavery – Southern Politics to 1860.* Columbia, SC. University of South Carolina Press. 2000.

Cox, Clinton. *Come All You Brave Soldiers – Blacks in the Revolutionary War.* New York, NY: Scholastic Inc. 2000.

Davis, Burke. *Black Heroes of the American Revolution.* New York, NY: Harcourt, Inc. 1976.

Edgerton, Robert B. *Hidden Heroism – Black Soldiers in America's Wars.* Boulder, CO: Westview Press. 2001.

Fleming, Thomas. *Liberty! The American Revolution.* New York, NY: Viking – The Penguin Group. 1997.

Fleming, Thomas. *Everybody's Revolution – A New Look at the People Who Won America's Freedom.* New York, NY: Scholastic Inc. 2006.

Helsley, Alexia Jones. *South Carolinians in the War for American Independence.* Columbia, SC: South Carolina Department of Archives and History. 2000.

Kaplan, Sidney and Emma Nogrady Kaplan. *The Black Presence in the Era of the American Revolution.* Amherst, MA: The University of Massachusetts Press. 1989.

Kochan, James L. (ill. By Don Troiani). *Soldiers of the American Revolution.* Mechanicsburg, PA: Stackpole Books. 2007.

Moss, Bobby G. and Michael Scoggins. *African-American Patriots in the Southern Campaign of the American Revolution.* Blacksburg, SC: Scotia-Hibernia Press. 2004.

Murray, Stuart A. P. *The American Revolution.* New York, NY: HarperCollins Publishers. 2006.

Nell, William C. *The Colored Patriots of the American Revolution.* Boston: Robert F. Walcutt. 1855.

Quarles, Benjamin. *The Negro in the American Revolution.* Chapel Hill, NC: University of North Carolina Press. 1961.

Savas, Theodore P. and J. David Dameron. *A Guide to the Battles of the American Revolution.* New York, NY: Savas Beatie LLC. 2006

Sedeen, Margaret. *Star-Spangled Banner – Our Nation and Its Flag.* Book Division of Washington, DC: The National Geographic Society. 1993.

Wood, W.J. *Battles of the Revolutionary War (1775-1781).* Cambridge, MA: Da Capo Press. 1990.